HOW TO OWN YOUR WORLD

...a Code for Taking the Path of the Spiritual Explorer

by
Stephen K. Hayes

Paperback: 978-1-955342-81-0
Hardcover: 978-1-955342-82-7

Stephen K. Hayes
PO Box 326
Bellbrook, OH 45305-0326
www.StephenKHayes.com

CONTENTS

HOW TO OWN YOUR WORLD

Forty years ago as a young man in my 30s, I found myself in a crisis. I was a career martial arts teacher, known for having brought the way of the ninja to the western world. This was before the ninja movies of the 1980s, Ninja Turtles, and a plethora of products from blenders to motorcycles to TV acrobat shows had usurped the ninja title.

A crazed and angry rival, claiming that he too had undergone secret ninja training, was jealous of my acclaim and frustrated with his lack of coverage. He ordered a few of his students to secretly travel to Ohio to kill me. That is what I was told by the Los Angeles county district attorney and the detectives he assigned to the case.

Stunned and alarmed, I realized I could not afford the security I needed. After several sleepless nights, I came up with a plan.

I would publicly take my wife and young daughters back to Japan, claiming I was returning for advanced training. I would then secretly double back to America, shave off my beard and don a blonde curly wig, and go out to California and put an end to that maniac.

Somehow in forging my desperate plan, it dawned on me just how far from reasonableness and morality I was willing to go to protect my family. Something in me had changed, something very wrong had taken me over. I reconsidered. I came up with a different idea.

My years of studying how to fight had somehow gotten me to where physical response to challenge was my first reaction. What I needed was spiritual balance. What I needed was a new mentor, one who could help me return to a truer direction in life.

I ended up journeying through Tibet, Nepal, and India, searching for a teacher with answers to my deepest questions. In an incredible twist of fate, in an almost unbelievable set of happenings, I ended up as a confidant of Tibet's Dalai Lama. I came to travel with him for years as his security escort. Complementing my background in the martial arts, I immersed myself in the spiritual sciences of Asia. Miraculously, I found the balance I had so intensely sought.

I am Stephen K. Hayes. Now in the later part of my life, I am amused to be referred to as everyone's image of the iconic master warrior sage. I am old. I am supposedly deadly. I am supposedly wise. Black Belt Magazine called me "*A legend; one of the ten most influential martial arts masters alive in the world today*".

Honestly, I followed my path over the decades as a way to better understand myself. I had no intention of being a teacher. And yet, as the years progressed, I more and more found myself in demand helping others through the knowledge I had gained. Somehow I was able to translate exotic esoteric concepts from ancient cultures into practical useful understanding for Western seekers. I eventually developed an ability to deliver a fuller approach to personal security and personal power.

So that is where this book came from. Its contents reflect in a stripped down blunt fashion just what I learned about life and the world as I traveled with the Dalai Lama.

To begin, let's start with a basic premise. You are a totally unique being in the world. Totally unique. Among the eight billion people on the planet, your fingerprints, your dental structure, your DNA sample can be used by even strangers to identify you exclusively, so unique is everything that makes you up.

And yet current culture tries to negate your uniqueness. It has become fashionable to downplay your individuality. You are now pigeonholed into a group identity, whether you like it or not.

You are labeled a wealthy black female, or an impoverished Asian child, or an elderly white male. Despite your absolute uniqueness, current culture wants to assign you an identity and further define you as oppressed or oppressor, victim or dominator, wronged or privileged.

What Are We Doing?

Tragically, if you forget about your uniqueness, you can so easily become convinced that life is a struggle with the world moving against your group in favor of other groups. This is a tragic trick being played on us to keep us fighting each other. We fail to pay attention to what the truly powerful are doing in the background.

OK, you may not agree with that world view. But can you agree that schools, religions, political parties, cultures, even sometimes parents and loved ones seem to have one idea of what you could or should be, and their definition may just be at odds with what you seek to experience deep down in your center?

Though I spent decades immersed in the Japanese and Tibetan cultures, I am very much a Western guy. I am a husband, father of two daughters, and grandfather of five. I ended up a writer, teacher, and most especially an ardent student of life. I am the author of over twenty books on how to apply the timeless knowledge of the East in contemporary Western life. Several of my volumes have been published in a variety of foreign languages.

I am committed to the idea that everyday Western people can gain much usefulness from these ancient codes. But those codes need to be translated into real English words. There is a tendency to make the teachings holy things, communicated in frustratingly obscure lofty language. But how is that going to help real people with real challenges? This secret knowledge needs to be translated into heart, mind, and gut recognizable terms.

How do you go about recognizing your uniqueness, and discovering your special purpose for being in the world? How do you recognize the vast possibilities working all around your life? How do you find and sing your song, discover your gift, and find your unique contribution? How do you break the spell of whatever stamps down on what truly makes you you?

My wife Rumiko and I blended what I studied with the grandmaster of the ninja and the Dalai Lama to create the practice of To-Shin Do. To-Shin Do is a contemporary mind and body self-protection and self-discovery system that is not limited to just martial arts. It is for Westerners. It is based on ancient ninja principles backed up by Himalayan codes for living in an authentic and elevated way. Everything has been updated and adapted for application to modern threats and pressures.

A Little History

The teacher that first offered the original form of this program lived over 2,500 years ago in Nepal and India. He became known as Shakyamuni, "Wise sage of the Shakya clan". He was also called "the Buddha", which means "one who has awakened to see the true nature of reality".

His approach to understanding how to make the most out of life was a spiritual revolution. He reversed the popular tendency to spend life wishing and hoping that something *outside* would change to where we could be happy on the *inside*. He focused on an *internal shift*, changing our mind and seeing things with a different vision. See with clarity from the *inside*, and you change your experience of the *outside*.

The Modern Purpose

Each one of us wants to be happy in their own unique way. Likewise, each one of us wants to avoid being unhappy. The unfortunate truth is that too often what we do in the hopes of finding happiness *actually* leads us towards the experience of confusion and heartache. Ironically, those thoughts and actions we work to avoid most often are exactly what we ought to do to bring ourselves peace and joy.

What if there were a tested plan for approaching authentic happiness, and moving away from the likelihood of experiencing unhappiness?

There is a disturbing increase in the number of people experiencing mental unwellness these days. With the exception of chronic depression, which requires medication to balance out the system, I might suggest that mental unfitness is a natural result of lifestyle choices, which seem to us not to be choices at all but inevitable prison sentences offered by our current culture.

If we could return to a life style of:

- Enjoyable daily heart-beating muscle-challenging exercise (not the point of this book)
- Eating a smaller diet of body-acceptable foods (for most of us, that means cutting out white stuff like sugar, pasta, breads, potatoes, milk; not the point of this book)
- Regularly ambling about enchanted in natural surroundings of woods, mountains, or seashore (not the point of this book)
- Spending as much time as possible with people we like and find meaning being around (I get this is admittedly difficult to pull off for working folks...)
- Focusing on upgrading the flawed habits of how we think and talk and show up (very much the point of this book)

...we could enjoy the heights of tip-top mental fitness and deep joy in life. We could reclaim our out-of-focus lives and maybe get an inkling that the universe indeed wants us to win. Get busy, get in the game, take joyful and committed responsibility for converting whatever is displeasing in your life.

What if there were a bedrock foundation of thoughts, actions, and expressions proven to better provide for the experience of clarity and understanding? What if your life could be lived authentically and to the fullest?

Wouldn't you be interested in exploring such a system if it were available?

How to Use the Program

This book is a way for you to understand the power of directed intention as a tool for accomplishment in all areas of life. Personal success, whether it be in the realms of physical, intellectual, economic, cultural, or spiritual breakthroughs, begins with a perception of potential.

We must work to cultivate a state of readiness, even fearlessness, in recognition of the reality that there will be times when things do not go the way we wish them to. We must then learn to live positively and generate the results we need in life by creating a *momentum of accomplishment*. This training program shows how to begin. It is then up to your own resourcefulness and commitment as to how far you take yourself.

This is a book of steps to take towards an experience of life characterized by clarity, depth, richness, and significance. Each page holds a thought to be considered, tested out, and even wrestled with or argued against.

Try reading each thought *out loud* slowly in a calm and clear voice. Take your time.

Experience the feel of each word.

Sure, it may feel weird or silly at first, reading these pages out loud, but try it and see what you get. Contemplate the meaning of what you hear when you speak each word. Be bold. Take a chance. Have fun.

Note new or fleeting impressions, memories, feelings, and ideas that flash across your mind as you speak the words.

Remember that this practice is a course correcting meditation. It is designed to facilitate clarity and advancement in your life, and counter confused thinking and off-center living. As time goes by, you may commit to memory some of the words of these sections, but by all means avoid thoughtless mechanical recitation.

Treat each repetition of this recitation practice as an exploration of who you are *right then and there that very day*.

If you are working with a group of friends, take turns

conducting the exercises. One person can sound a small bell or clap two pieces of wood together and read aloud the introductory words while the others listen in meditative awareness with eyes partially closed. All then join in voicing aloud the points of recitation.

If possible, use one ring of a bell or snap of the clappers to physically and mentally punctuate:

- Announcement of the name and description of the exercise
- Completion of the recitation of each section of the exercise
- Final eventual completion of the contemplation of each exercise

Question every word of the recitation. Consider what new insights are evoked each time you read the words. The words may appear simple and unchanging, but you are a different person from day to day.

Look at your feelings summoned by the words. Are you inspired, angered, encouraged, depressed, egged on, or doubtful? Critical thinking is encouraged!

Reflect on your actual daily actions, words, and intentions. Compare those with what is recommended by the practice.

Based on your *actual* thoughts, feelings, comments, behavior, and the way you live each day right now, what do you *really* believe you know about life?

From knowledge of who you are and how you are living *right now*, how would you like to grow? Where would you like to go as the future becomes your present? More wealth... or more simplicity? More peace... or more intensity? More connection... or more self-contentment?

Strive to keep in mind a promise to:

- Recognize that *fulfillment is possible*, and then...
- Learn to *apply the technologies*, in order to...
- Achieve the *freedom of personal advancement*

Five Secret Goals

Work to discover what brings you closer to the five qualities of a life fully lived. This is laid out in exotic Indian, Tibetan, and Japanese *mandala* blueprint maps for spiritual actualization, but it is pretty simple. We all want:

Authority

A sense of being worthy of accessing life's great abundance; to be in charge of accomplishing our own goals, and to know that we set our own boundaries.

We want to be important.

Knowledge

Authentic understanding of who we are and what is true about life; to realize what is real, and to attain personal peace through intelligence.

We want to be right.

Connection

Kinship with community and the hearts of others; to express who we really are, and to share respect, admiration, and love with others.

We want to be appreciated.

Service

A sense of engagement with the adventure process of life; to expand brightness and good over negative, and to know that we are a part of something bigger than self.

We want to be needed.

Personal Fulfillment

Experience of enlightened peace that comes with wisdom; a sense of having the space to live up to our dreams and expectations.

We want to experience the significance of why we are alive.

My Secret Message for Generating Success...

In the final chapter of this book, I will impart what I consider to be the ultimate secret to success, vibrant mental health, being needed and revered by people, generating sufficient income, and creating a life where you are poised and ready for something wild and unexpected that will take you upward to meaning and significance - to making your indelible mark.

Is any of this striking a chord, making you curious, egging you on to see what all of this is about? Are you willing to give it a shot? Let's begin...

SEEKER'S CREED
Preparing for the Path

What you need more than anything else in the beginning is a firm foundation as to what you expect of yourself. Others may offer different opinions. You need to cut through all of that and determine where *you* need to go.

When taking on any dangerous experience, there are three areas where you need to be absolutely certain. It is just too risky to jump in and see what comes along. You want to be certain you have what it takes to succeed, believe totally in your preparation, and have the reassurance that others have succeeded and can mentor you as you attempt the risky adventure.

This seems simple, but it may just be a secret. Experience shows that the common enemies of the spirit encountered by all of us at various times in life are:

- **False ideals**

  ...wrong thoughts and beliefs about your capabilities that breed lack of self-confidence

- **False creeds**

  ...following flawed paths of thought and behavior that lead away from success and breed confusion

- **False friends**

  ...hanging around the wrong people who urge on your cynicism and doubt

What we need more than anything else in the beginning are

- **Noble ideals**
- **Workable plans**
- **True allies**

Promise yourself that you will make a commitment to awakening the potential for living life fully. Your promise taps into the potential inherent in the three treasures of:

- **Confidence**

  ...for noble ideals

a whole new concept of
    what you can become

- **Discipline**

  ...for workable plans

a whole new range of
    what you can learn and master

- **Respect**

  ...for worthy allies

a whole new community of
    friends and teachers

I believe in myself.

I am confident.

I can accomplish my goals.

Start with a pledge to wake up and activate the highest potential within you.

The three-part seeker's creed is a reminder to live up to your capacity as an explorer and doer in life.

If you do not believe in your potential for accomplishment, you are defeated before you even begin.

Have you ever known someone who did not believe in himself or herself?

Watching them, perhaps even trying to encourage them on and then encountering their resistance, you learned that motivation can only come from within.

I believe in what I study.

I am disciplined.

I am ready

to learn and advance.

To grow is to change.

When you have changed very much, it means that you have grown very much.

When you are inspired by following the ages-old ideal of knowing more about what is *really true* about life, you are just naturally drawn towards that which will encourage growth.

Even at the expense of letting go of old and familiar cherished beliefs and limitations, you can not help but be motivated to explore on.

I believe in my teachers.

I show respect for all

who help me progress.

Think of all the people who have helped you along by providing encouragement, advice, support, and a living example of how to get what you know you deserve.

A good teacher is a treasure in your life. Even the greatest of all champions have coaches and trainers they rely on to bring out the best in them.

A truly powerful person is comfortable acknowledging the accomplishments and worthiness of others. Extend respect to get respect. To salute and repay all those who cared enough to help you grow, be a great practitioner and encourage others in turn.

MINDFUL ACTION
Defining the Path

There are fourteen specific bad habits that account for most of the self-induced misery in the world. One or more of these fourteen bad habits sadly make up the basis of all crimes committed, loving relationships broken, jobs failed, friendships ruined, and nations going to war against each other.

Stretching across all times and cultures, these fourteen weaknesses are so easy to slip into, despite their proven inability to generate positive results.

Use this code of mindful action to avoid having to make important life-quality decisions quickly under pressure. You have already made up your mind as to how you will handle things before they appear in your life. Prepare now.

It is OK to question each of the 14 points as to its truth. Earn these. Make every day a practice of transcending unconscious auto-pilot or power abdicating "sleep-walk" living. Take charge. Wake up.

I protect life and health.

I avoid violence

whenever possible.

Develop your ability to serve as a protector, so that wherever you go, everyone is a little safer and more secure because you are there.

The world already has too many predators.

Retaliating with even more cruelty will not solve your problems.

Whenever possible, be bigger than the pull of petty vengeance and violence.

Make the world a safer place for all.

I respect

the property

and space

of all.

I avoid

taking

what has not been offered.

Stealing money, resources, ideas, loyalties, and credit eats away at your own sense of personal worth.

Do not degenerate to the level of a lowly parasite, feeding off the efforts of others who work to produce value in the world.

Look around for what you can do to be of such value to others that you thereby generate legitimately all that you need.

I develop

significant relationships.

I avoid

abusing others

for selfish gain.

Do not treat others' hearts in a reckless way.
Do not use others heartlessly.

Encourage significance, empowerment, and trust through authentic friendship.

Users, abusers, seducers, rapists, and con artists demean the beauty of that which they twist into use for their own pleasure.

Model your relationships on the way you would want others to treat

your parents

or your children.

I thoughtfully express the truth.

I avoid

the confusion

of dishonest words.

Be real.

No one respects a phony.

No one wants to invest time in a fake.

Lying to yourself and others makes it impossible to live with integrity, and you will not impress people for long.

Liars are at best annoying and pathetic, and at the most destructive and damaging.

Be sure that your words match your actions, and your actions match your words.

I cultivate

a positive attitude,

a healthy body,

and a clear mind.

I avoid

whatever would reduce

my physical or mental

well-being.

Do not mistreat yourself.

It is easy to get hooked on destructive and addictive distractions that lead away from clear and directed consciousness. Alcohol, nicotine, drugs, and even food or affection can lure us into a false illusion of contentment with life.

Avoid escapes from clarity.

Enjoy the vibrant health that results from facing life square on.

I communicate

health,

happiness,

and peace of mind

to everyone I meet.

I avoid

violent, disturbing,

and unduly critical speech.

To compete with the savage noisy clamor that dominates so much of our lives, you can be tempted to match the sheer volume and harshness with your own voice.

Severe criticism of others can suggest fear and insecurity on the part of the critic.

Bold talk without real action is cheap.

Use assuring and positive words to encourage others, and reconcile and resolve any conflicts.

I promote harmony

and positive momentum

to bring out

the best in everyone.

I avoid

causing alienation,

doubt,

and division

among others.

No one respects a troublemaker, back-stabber, or two-faced two-timer.

Putting down others to build yourself up just adds more negative energy to an already fractured world.

Work to build a reputation of being one who builds and encourages positive momentum in other people's lives.

I encourage all

to speak purposefully

from the heart.

I avoid

the dull contentment

of gossip

and small talk.

Avoid the nervous habit of talking on with fluffy chatter as a means of filling in silence or hiding from your true feelings and observations.

Do not spread stories you do not know to be fact. Avoid whisper campaigns that have the sole purpose of hurting others.

Speak with grounded words from the heart, or purposefully withhold speech and save your energy if that better expresses the needs of the moment.

I am as enthusiastic

about others' fulfillment

as I am about my own.

I avoid

treating others' successes

as the cause

of my lacks.

Resenting or envying what others have created undermines your own self-esteem.

You do not need that.

Do not delude yourself into thinking of others as "lucky" and yourself as not. Rejoice in the good fortune of others. If there is one more happy person in your world, you now live in a happier world. There is one more example of positive potential there for you and everyone else.

I promote the enjoyment of life, and encourage others

with my smile.

I avoid

setting myself

against the world.

Hostility, anger, and maliciousness are easy habits to develop.

See them as the traps they are.

Bring ease to your life.

Be kind to yourself.

Show strength by choosing compassion.

Look for ways to improve the quality of others' days, thereby improving your experience of the world you inhabit.

I strive

for the personal realization

of truth.

I avoid

the seductive comfort of

narrow-mindedness.

Operating from a set of beliefs or principles that do not match authentic reality makes life confusing and hard to endure.

Strive to look beyond your own personal "conventional truth" to realize the grander timeless "ultimate truth" that underpins all of our experiences.

Focus more on coming up with new questions than defending old answers.

I accomplish

what must be done

in a timely

and effective way.

I avoid

putting off

what will benefit me

and my world

today.

You never get a "day off" from life.

Do it now.

Enjoy making each precious moment count
for something.

I strive to be so strong

that nothing

can disturb

my peace of mind.

I avoid

the negative effects of

worry,

doubt,

and regret.

Be cheerful and optimistic.

Look for the brightness and value in every encounter and experience.

Vow to create a life in which you find yourself too big for worry, too majestic for doubt, too grand for anger, and too strong for fear.

I work to build

love, happiness,

and loyalty

among all members

of my family.

I avoid

putting temporary

personal benefit

ahead of the welfare

of those I love.

Skillfully express your appreciation and encouragement to each family member every day. You know what they want to hear.

No other success can justify failure in the home.

LIFE'S FOUR TRUTHS

The Way It Is

Life is bound to hurt as long as we go through our days with a set of expectations, beliefs, and hopes that do not match up with the actual workings of what is ultimately true.

The big truth is that life is full of things, people, qualities, experiences, encounters, and conclusions that we wish with all our heart...

would have
should have
could have
been different.

The question is not *whether* you will encounter heartbreak, disappointment, sorrow, illness and death as a part of life, but rather *how* you are going to handle it when you do.

The world is full of prejudice, cruel humor, snobbery, bad service, shoddy workmanship, mediocre performances, unfair advantages, and the timeless tendency for the ones with social, economic, or cultural power to protect their ability to exclude the ones without it.

Sure, we strive nobly to "think positively", but sometimes the innocents suffer and the bad guys win. Sometimes the truly valiant are brushed aside and the callous and calculating are praised and rewarded.

Acceptance of such a realization comes from dispassionate recognition, and not at all from pessimism. It is a positive observation to note that the power of negativity is an awesome truth of life. Truly, it is the way of nature for things to fall down and break up. An entire boxcar of crisp red apples will be taken to ruin by the one tiny rotten core. The combined goodness of all the fresh apples is powerless to bring the rotten one back to purity.

It is the way of life for people to create their own suffering by insisting that harmful things make them feel good, and that truly beneficial things bring them down. Without opening the eye of enlightened vision, we are doomed to carry into each new generation the mistaken opinions of all the ill informed people who, entirely through accident, contributed towards making us who we are today. We forget to consider the fact that had different people and experiences influenced our backgrounds, we would be entirely different individuals. Reality as we know it would be radically different. We then fight and argue to protect and promote those very limitations that cause us all the heartache.

Such a mindset is called ignorance.

Though often difficult to accept, it is through fully embracing the laws of nature that we are led to the attainment of ultimate peace of mind. Be brave enough to look at life as it is. Search through all the illusions. Come to understand that "what is" really depends upon our own interpretation.

Such a mindset is called intelligence.

Be insightful enough to cheerfully share with all others your knowledge of the methods for discovering truth. Know that assisting others is the most powerful thing you can do to promote your own best interests.

Such a mindset is called compassion.

Use every experience you encounter to broaden your understanding of how life really works.

Such a mindset is called wisdom.

**The truth is
that every life
includes difficulties
that lead to
stress and anxiety.**

Every single one of us goes through times where life seems to be a rough ride.

Heartbreak

Separation from what you love

Encountering what you wish to avoid

Illness

Growing old

Death

...are inescapable parts of life. They come with the package. Even the most pampered of celebrities has their gripes. No one can evade. No amount of wishing, hoping, scheming, or praying can make the laws of nature reverse themselves "just this once" for you.

That's the truth.

The truth is

that we experience

stress and anxiety

because

we desire

life to be

what it can not be.

Suffering comes from hoping we are correct in our beliefs about how life "ought to be", and then being surprised and disappointed by the reality that life just isn't fair when judged by the standard of what we believe.

When we chase after the impossible and run from the inevitable in hopes that life will give us a break, we are pouring energy into a hopeless cause.

That's the truth.

The truth is

that cause and effect

is the process by which

difficulty

produces stress and anxiety

... and

awakened living

produces peace of mind.

Look at what you did in the past to know
why things are the way they are today.

Look at what you are doing today to know
how things will be in the future.

Life operates on a scientific basis of causes
producing effects.

Effects in turn become new causes that in
turn produce new effects.

That's the truth.

**The truth is
that difficulty
is overcome
by paying attention to
how you live your life
from one moment to the next.**

Since causes produce effects, decide to take charge of those causes and create the effects you want to experience.

Choose your path with purpose in mind.

Replace those

thought patterns

behaviors

expressions

that lead to anguish and distress, and you are on your way to eliminating suffering.

That's the truth.

ACOMPLISHMENT PLAN
Eight Steps to Success

All of us have our dreams. Whenever dreams are turned into reality, a group of eight specific personal activators are almost always present in the process. Conversely, lack of these eight qualities accounts for the vast majority of failures to create what we need in life.

Learn how to gain control of the process by which you create your future.

Promise yourself to observe the eight steps of the accomplishment plan as a method for turning

dreams into goals,

goals into objectives,

objectives into tasks,

and tasks into steps

to produce what you need.

Yep. There is a formula for creating success.

Ultimate truth is ultimate!

I see life

as it really is

and stay tuned in!

Verify it!

Allow yourself to develop a proper mindset.

Proper perspective is the most important asset you bring to your personal quest for a fulfilling life.

Be ready to change your mind about the way you believe things are.

The ultimate secret is that nothing

really is

the way we think it looks.

Seek out everything that can expand your perspective on the true significance of the experience of life.

Let all you encounter serve to guide you towards advancing wholeness.

Are you ready for that?

I take charge of inner vision

and set my mind on

what I need to see!

Visualize it!

Simply think a thing

...and you create its reality.

The subconscious mind is programmed through repeated input. Be mindful.

With a positive and healthy attitude, your thoughts just naturally guide your speech and actions towards proper constructive progress.

Vow to create an inner vision of only that which you wish to experience.

I communicate truth

and say

what I need to hear!

Verbalize it!

What the subconscious mind encounters
over and over again

becomes the core of its contents.

What you hear often enough

becomes the reality

that you experience around you.

Be precise.

Speak what you seek.

I work constructively

to generate

what I need to experience!

Vitalize it!

When the world sees you going about the business of living in a way consistent with your inner vision and expressed intention, then the world presumes that life experience to be your reality.

The world figures that if you...

Look like a happy enlightened being,

Think like a happy enlightened being,

Sound like a happy enlightened being,

Deal with others

like a happy enlightened being,

...then...

You must be a happy enlightened being.

I take responsibility

for what surrounds me

in the world!

Vantage!

Examine all your choices.

If your days are filled with negative encounters, it is because somehow you have chosen to live around negative people.

If your days are filled with negative events, it is because somehow you have chosen to live in negative surroundings.

If your days are filled with negative actions, it is because somehow you have chosen to live with negative occupations.

If you do not take responsibility for the influences that shape your life, who will?

Make the choice to make a choice.

I keep

positive momentum going

and make

the right things happen!

Valor!

Some are known as

dreamers of great dreams.

Others awaken and get to work.

Courage

Enthusiasm

Diligence

will be required of those championing the
triumph of

intelligence

compassion

and wisdom.

Get moving! Do it!

I use every experience

as an opportunity to grow.

Everything matters!

Vigilance!

Every moment has its lesson.

Stay mindful of all the possibilities.

What is the higher value of what you are experiencing

Right now?

Right now?

Right now?

What is there to learn and enjoy

Right here?

Right here?

Right here?

Each and every encounter experienced

...could provide the final piece of the puzzle that lifts us to enlightened peace of spirit.

Consistent concentration!

I center my spirit

right *here*

right *now!*

Veracity!

Take the time to practice paying attention to paying attention.

Watch from the inside out in a calm, clear, and scientific manner.

Practice being mindful even when you think you do not need to be mindful.

Beyond all hopes and habits, who are you?

Look at how you appear.

Talk about how you speak.

Ponder over how you think.

Develop the habit of questioning all habits.

SIX HEROIC PARAMETERS

Living the Noble Life

The hero holds firm to the ideal of making the world a better place by courageously putting self-interest aside to assist others, even in the face of overwhelming danger or at cost of great personal sacrifice.

The heroic in life are inspired, guided, and motivated to improve the world and help make life better for all by means of personally cultivated:

- Knowledge - direct experiential connection with highest truth, recognizing the true nature of reality...

    ...and

- Compassion - the wish that all might have the opportunity to experience such life-changing empowering insights.

As part

of my every

thought,

word,

and action,

I am inspired

by the heroic ideal of

generously caring for others.

I want to make the world

a better place!

Contrary to the tempting pull of greed, think of how great it would feel to be so strong that anything anyone needed to brighten a life, you could easily supply it while enhancing your own experience of life at the same time.

As part

of my every

thought,

word,

and action,

I am inspired

by the heroic ideal of

ethical discipline

as I pursue my goals.

I live my principles!

Contrary to the tempting pull of self-doubt, vow to take a stand in the world.

Living your code in the face of opposition is what makes heroism so heroic.

As part

of my every

thought,

word,

and action,

I am inspired

by the heroic ideal of

tolerant *patience.*

I do not

take opposition personally!

There are forces in the world that do not want brightness and wholeness to prevail.

The greater your commitment to truth and compassion, the more opposition you will generate.

Do not be tempted by anger. Do not fall prey to discouragement.

Be calm. Be focused. Be ready.

As part

of my every

thought,

word,

and action,

I am inspired

by the heroic ideal of

courageous diligent *effort*.

I work to make things happen!

Campaigning against the dark forces of cruelty, fear, and selfishness is hard and demanding work.

Ready to roll up your sleeves and get dirty, and maybe take a few thumps?

Some things are worth fighting for.

It will never be easier, so jump in now.

As part

of my every

thought,

word,

and action,

I am inspired

by the heroic ideal of

concentrated *awareness.*

I am in the moment

here

now!

Pay attention to staying alert.

Nothing doesn't matter.

As part

of my every

thought,

word,

and action,

I am inspired

by the heroic ideal of

knowing highest *truth*.

I keep sight of the big picture!

There is a timeless deepest *universal truth* stretching from past to present to future.

There is as well a conventional *personal truth* that interprets experience to create memories that lead to the formation of beliefs.

Study and practice to make the ultimate truth more and more your personal truth.

SIX VIEWS OF LIFE

Transforming the Illusion

The hero's life is a journey through the "six realms of hopes and dreams".

The true hero is on a noble quest to empower others towards the higher experience of the significance of life. That can only come from upgraded vision.

Life seems overwhelming to the unenlightened. They believe in their stubborn desire to see as highest truth their own flawed and habitually deluded ideas of how life should work.

Individuals can unwittingly become trapped in one of six psychological states of existence.

Pierce through the illusion.

Dismantle the delusion.

Cultivate from the roots of negativity the blossom of wisdom.

Those who believe that

life is hell

live hellish lives

full of anger, hatred,

and alienation.

Habitual

cold estrangement from others

can be transformed

into the wisdom of

cool scientific observation.

From the

enlightened perspective of

seeking *knowledge*,

I know that

distance and investigative curiosity

leads to *intelligence*!

Those who believe that

there is not enough

live like greedy and desperate

hungry wretches.

Habitual

frantic craving for satisfaction

can be transformed

into the wisdom of

warm compassionate

discerning insight!

From the

enlightened perspective of

appreciating *interconnection*,

I know that

expressing regard for others

leads to receiving *respect*!

Those who believe that

life is confusing

live ignorant lives full of

delusion and helplessness.

Habitual

dull and fuzzy thinking

can be transformed

into the wisdom of

accommodating all

within the big picture!

From the

enlightened perspective of

awakening *personal responsibility*,

I know that

conscious attention

leads to *broadness of vision*!

Those who believe that

life can be ruled and
restrained

live frustrating lives

dependent upon

that which ever changes.

Habitual clinging to

the comfortably familiar

can be transformed

into the wisdom of

authentic peace of mind!

From the

enlightened perspective of

exercising *acceptance*,

I know that

non-attachment

leads to *freedom*!

Those who believe that

their insecurity

is the fault of those they envy

live rootless competitive lives

full of suspicion and self-doubt.

Habitual uncertainty

***can* be transformed**

into the wisdom of

efficiently accomplishing

whatever must be done.

From the

enlightened perspective of

cultivating *usefulness*,

I know that

serving others

leads to a sense of *being needed*!

Those who believe that

only they are of value

live arrogant egotistical lives

acting as gods above all others.

Habitual

narrow minded self-limitation

can be transformed

into the wisdom of

appreciating the value

of all things

and experiences.

From the

enlightened perspective of

appreciating *abundance,*

I know that

humble gratitude

leads to *happiness!*

MEDITATION

Calm Mind – Centered Spirit

The Key to Productivity

It is a common thing to forget how easily stress can creep in and take root in our daily routine. Tension and rigidity then become permanent fixtures in our lives. It becomes a habit to remain all locked in to keeping pace with the demands of a workday with too much to do in too few hours. We know that high-pressure living pushes physical and mental health to the frayed edge, but what can we do about it?

Cultivate the habit of meditation as a means of breaking the spell of labored momentum. Ironically, you will find that a few breaks in the daily activity will actually provide *more* in terms of productivity than sustaining the forced pace even after creativity and energy have been used up.

Make arrangements for a ten minute meditative revitalization break between breakfast and lunch, and then again between lunch and dinner. At first you may feel guilty, knowing there is "so much to be done." Make a commitment nonetheless. Persevere and look for the rewards you will gather. Do it. You are worth it.

Practice some form of meditative revitalization every day. You can train or refresh the mind through:

- Awareness concentration
- Thought investigation
- Hoped-for results visualization

As a beginning meditation, stretch your back and major muscles and take your meditation seat in a chair or on a cushion. Settle in and straighten your back. Be very aware of good healthy posture. Do not slouch or fall back. If you are leading a meditation session with others, ring the bowl gong or snap two blocks of wood together...

1.   One time to signal the *physical* settling-in as you prepare for meditation. Stretch, breathe deeply, and get centered.

2.   A second time to signal *mental* settling-in. Close your eyes. Scan your senses for cues from the surrounding area and from within.

3.   A third time to signal the shifting of consciousness inward to the center of *meditative awareness*. This is the start of the real practice itself. Watch the breath come in and go out of your center. Allow yourself to become the watching process.

4.   When you reach the point of feeling that the *space* around you is less crowded or compact, and that time has softened its control and urgency, you are going deeper into the actual meditative state.

5.   Use a string of counter beads as a timing device to monitor the exercise. Move your thumb up and down over one bead at a time in coordination with the *in* and *out* breath. Breathe in and slide your thumb up one side of a bead. Breathe out and slide your thumb down the other side of the bead. That is one breath cycle. Keep going one bead at a time until you bump into the large center bead. Practice and see how many beads it takes for you to do five minutes, nine minutes, fifteen minutes, or twenty minutes. Count back and away from the large center bead and start in from that point.

6.   Pick something to hold in mind, and enjoy the practice

of returning your consciousness to that, whenever your mind wanders off (and it *will* wander off...). You can be fascinated with your breath moving in and out. You can be fascinated with your slowly expanding presence in the room. You can be fascinated by a forward (or backward!) counting of numbers. You can be fascinated by your ever-settling base and ever-rising upright posture. You can be fascinated by repeating an encouraging phrase over and over, such as, "Relax" or "Energized" or "Joyous" or "Right here, right now" or "I am home".

7.   At the end of the practice session, a single light sounding of the gong gently signals the reverse of the three steps for the return from meditative consciousness to outward awareness. Stretch gently and open your eyes. Feels great, doesn't it?

SPIRITUAL FOCUS

Life's Highest Purpose

In our role as human beings, our most important work is the attainment of spiritual illumination.

Once it dawns on us that such expansion *is possible*, we can never turn away or retreat from the quest. We are compelled to explore on after the highest goal - liberation from the confusion and heartbreak of a life characterized by impossibly futile wishes and hopes and dreams.

With singularity of heart
I openly acknowledge
and express
my awe
for the ten-directions
and ten-dimensions
of unfathomable mystery revealed
as the infinite timeless universe,
the true essential nature of which manifests and
teaches itself
through the eternally unchanging
realization process accessed by exploring the Three
Treasures:

1. My innermost potential
to be discovered and fulfilled;

2. The authentic method
for actualization of that potential;

3. The demonstrated proof
of that potential and that method
working in the lives of those who
have taken the path before me.

May I be firm
in my determination
to pursue the study of truth,
and never give in to weariness
no matter how long
I must follow the quest.

(Clasp your hands together in front of your chest, and call upon the ancient nine syllable vow, translated as, "Here warriors all lined bold in front" to summon the nine protective powers of a fully actualized human being.)

RIN
To be strong and vital, unhindered
in body, mind, and spirit

PYO
To activate and actualize the brightness potential in all the energy centers of my body

TOH
To follow my true path with authentic ease, and avoid extreme diversions born from seeds of depression, frivolity, and

dullness

SHA
To be whole and happy and radiantly healthy, and to be free from illness, injury, and incapacitation

KAI
To be safe and secure, and to evade effortlessly the damaging effects of distress, misfortune, obstruction, and dark influence

JIN
To follow the directives of the bright way, rather than be pulled by the tempting whisper of divisive passions; to receive the guidance of the divine scheme of totality

RETS'
To reach through the vastness of endless time and infinite space to access highest wisdom

ZAI
To attain enlightenment as to the major questions of my life,
...generating the *diamond* legacy of exploring highest truth
...and the *lotus* legacy of assisting all beings to realize truth

ZEN
To vanish from the sight of all that is divisive and diminishing, and rise from the dark and teeming confusion of birth and death to realize the direct experience of oneness with all.

May I be neither too ill nor suffering at the time of my passing away to know of its approach by at least several days,
    so that I may focus my thoughts
    peacefully and properly
    on universal brightness,
    gently letting go of this body,

unattached by any ties
at the last moment,
to emerge at once in the realm of highest brightest truth,
to encounter the grace of divinity
face to face
and experience final realization of supreme illumination,
thereby enabling me to expand infinitely
throughout the realm of formless ultimate truth,
and generate the momentum of that which will help all
beings rise from the teeming ocean of cycles of birth and death.

I offer these petitions for blessing to all brightening and
enlightened forces
in the past, present, and future,
here, there, and everywhere,
in all ten directions
and ten dimensions
of the boundless universe,
in the spirit of crossing over
to the peace that exceeds all understanding,
the direct realization of highest transcendent supreme
wisdom.

FIVE PROTECTIONS

Spiritual Armor for the Quest

All phenomena, experiences, and things are derived from the same essentially pure source potential.

Limitless potential must be essentially pure because it is impossible to imagine something from *outside the universe* having a role in any reality we create.

Therefore, I know that I too must be made up of essential purity of potential.

As essential purity embodied, I create my own experiences by means of my

actions

words

intentions

In the past, because I did not know any better, I made my life difficult by means of unskillful actions, words, and intentions that I *believed* to be effective in taking me towards what I thought I wanted. This caused me and others to drift further into the tragic deluded illusion that life is made up of separate and competing entities.

In truth, all of life is a constant flow of interrelated changing conditions and forms. As individuals, we remember impressions of what we think our experiences were. We each in our own way interpret as our own unique stories the universal experience of

timeless
    infinite
        formless
            essentially pure
                source potential.

I can create the reality I wish to experience by being mindful to guide those ever-changing conditions and forms towards the opportunity to realize directly the wholeness and unity of the universe.

This moment

in this place

is the birth

of my opportunity

to create

the reality I experience.

Ah-ha!

Timeless eternity expresses itself in the experience of a series of countless present moments of who you are. See this moment move from *then* to *now* into the *future*.

Gently let go of all you believe to be the defining characteristics of your identity and personality at this point. You are so much bigger than how others define and limit you.

You can be anything you set your mind on.

Infinite timelessness here in this moment!

I create

the reality I experience

through

enlightened action.

Imagine a perfect role model demonstrating perfection of effortless effective presence.

One movement...

and worlds change for the better.

Imagine that heroic role model passing their secret to your innermost core of being.

You become the essence of enlightened graceful bearing in the world.

See your body surrounded by a flare of brilliant white light.

Oh! Presence!

I create

the reality I experience

through

enlightened communication.

Imagine a perfect role model demonstrating perfection of effortless effective speech.

One word...

and worlds change for the better.

Imagine that heroic role model passing their secret to your innermost core of being.

You become the essence of enlightened moving and connecting communication.

See your words grace others like the touch of soft red lotus blossom petals.

Ah! Connection!

I create

the reality I experience

through

enlightened intention.

Imagine a perfect role model demonstrating perfection of effortless effective intention.

One thought...

and worlds change for the better.

Imagine that heroic role model passing their secret to your innermost core of being.

You become the essence of enlightened thought generating reality.

See your mind reflect highest actuality like a cool blue diamond mirror.

Hmm! Truth!

I am shielded

by the armor

of universal brightness

as I battle

the grim dragons of

fear

and ignorance.

The corrupting triple-poison powers of desperation, discord, and delusion will feel threatened by your brightness.

See yourself clad in the rainbow-reflecting crystal armor of mindfulness, surrounded by an orb of bright purifying light, a sword gripped in one hand to cut through delusion and a rope lariat coiled in the other to pull back those fearing the challenge of advancement.

Ho! Perseverance!

DEDICATING BENEFIT

Be a Blessing in the World

Each of us wants to be of value and significance and positive influence in the world of which we are a part.

Therefore, we are pulled to take up these wisdom attainment practices.

Advancing towards the holiness of wholeness

...is the highest and most noble obligation of the human being.

As a consequence of the strength of our pure intentions in this practice,

...and through any advancement that our practice may generate,

...we wish with all our heart, mind, and body

...that our world may be a better place.

We dedicate the benefits of our work not to small personal satisfaction,

...but to the advancement of the entire spectrum of energies that makes up

...the world that we know

...and have yet to know.

As we revel in the touch of love and friendship sent our way,

...may we will such kindness on to all others immeasurably.

As we appreciate the help of those who assist us in times of trouble,

...may we will such compassion on to all others immeasurably.

As we delight in the direct experience of all the wonders of a life fully lived,

...may we will such joy on to all others immeasurably.

As we honor the gift of understanding that results from broadness of vision,

...may we will such peace of mind on to all others immeasurably.

May we be of positive influence
...in the universal experience
...shared by all.
May the cycles of nature
...provide for all an abundance of
...sustenance and prosperity
...so that all beings in all lands
...may secure the means to live in
...peace and dignity,
...thereby permitting all to discern the inclination towards the pursuit of light.
May all beings
...be led to the freedom
...of awakening to supreme wisdom.
May the radiant glory of highest truth
...illuminate the world
...to banish confusion and distress.
May our work be auspicious.
May wholeness,
significance, and virtue
...be promoted in every way.

GAN NI SHI KU DOKU

May all merit and benefit generated by this work

FU GYU O IS-SAI

be extended to aid all beings

GA TO YO SHU JO

so that we along with all others

KAI GU JO BUTSU DO

may attain the way

of supreme awakening.

AUTHOR'S SOURCES
for
How To Own Your World

My own code of "how to own the world" is the result of exposure to so many powerful influences in addition to the lore of that original great teacher who lived south of the Himalayas almost three thousand years ago.

My father Ira M. Hayes reminded me of the blunt truth, *"It's almost impossible not to be more successful or happy if you really want to be."* His philosophy was to say "Great!" no matter what happened, and everything was great when compared with all the lesser possibilities.

My spiritual role model Tenzin Gyatso, the Dalai Lama of Tibet, reminded me to keep my focus on the highest of ideals. His core message was *"Develop intelligence and demonstrate that as kindness."* Through amazing twists of fate, I found the Dalai Lama as spiritual ideal, and then set up my life to be available to gain the lessons at his side.

My wife Rumiko was a living example of grace and peace throughout our life together. Like my own mother Carolyn before her, Rumiko's was a life of service and caring, so her husband could roam the world challenging the dragons of fear and ignorance. I encourage my daughters to live more like their mother and grandmother, and less like their father.

My martial arts teacher Masaaki Hatsumi cautioned me that the bigger my work grew in significance, and the more well-known I became, the more people would jealously come to resent my success and stature. The greater and brighter the cause, the more bitter the enemies attracted.

One final note to those tempted to comment with scowling lips and furrowed brow that the program in this book is a very material-worldly approach to spiritual cultivation...

Yes, it is,

...and thank you so much for noticing.

Please share this volume with those friends for whom such a program would be just the right - *and quite possibly the only acceptable* - introduction to spiritual exploration.

Be happy. Find peace. Do great things.

For information on training in the disciplines shared by
Stephen K. Hayes, contact him at:

Stephen K. Hayes
PO Box 326
Bellbrook, OH 45305-0326 USA
hombu@to-shin-do.com
www.StephenKHayes.com

How To Own Your World

This book offers a powerful and useful program for examining the role of the individual in the complexity of the grand unfolding experience of life. Author Stephen K. Hayes draws upon experiences with key sources from his life-long quest for insights, in order to compile this clear and direct statement of the ideal for the seeker of self-mastery.

Sections include considerations on ethics, truths about heroic living, spiritual aspiration and meditation. In extremely straightforward English, *How To Own Your World* presents truths for grasping the ancient and modern wisdom of the world in a form readily accessible to the modern seeker.

www.ingramcontent.com/pod-product-compliance
Lightning Source LLC
Chambersburg PA
CBHW051317120626
46547CB00015B/2277